DIVISION STREET

POETRY BY

C.K. FLACH

Palmetto Publishing Group, LLC
Charleston, SC

For information regarding special discounts or for bulk purchases, please contact Palmetto Publishing Group at Info@PalmettoPublishingGroup.com.

ISBN-13: 978-1-944313-08-1
ISBN-10: 1-944313-08-7

PRELUDE

Inhale
Exhale
Again now, my sweet one
Release your thoughts
To the daydreams beckoning
Quickly now, child
The vapor knows best
Filling your lungs like a sanctified messenger
Give us this day our daily breath
Oh, yellow agent
Show me the future
Teach me so I might see

CHAPTER I

Isn't this where we came in?
(Enter passageway)
Have a seat; someone will be with you shortly…

To dream undisturbed
        Unthreatened
                By the dawn

Calling out to a vacant scene,
Where are my dreamers?
Searching for new life
Beneath a labyrinth of stars
Distant & polite

War paint & a new moon
Poised to survive
Your solitude, your carelessness
A generous guide

The bill has already been handled,
Paid for by blood currency
Beneath a blood moon
On a dry hill of skulls

Take that bandage off
Let the wound breathe
Administer revival
Do you recall eternity?

Silver-mine clouds
Soft, vibrant sheets of childhood
Evil abounds
Sacrament
Sacrilege
Scrutiny
All hammering down

Chains forged
In hell's maelstrom
Dying to become wisdom
& more

CHAPTER II

The City
Mighty ambassador
To the land of idols
Ambitions
Virtues
Opinions displayed on billboards

Sidewalks
Street preachers
Neon signs
Casinos

Peasants & orphans line the wounded streets
Calculating gamblers
Dig graves with the ace of spades
"I'm tired of taking the train," she announced,
Cigarette burning her fingertips
The iron mill is stagnant
No smoke over there
Boxer's battle bare-knuckled
While a parade moves softly by
This is wonderful news
This is the city that God forgot

CHAPTER III

"I did my hair for you," she mentions timidly
Hoping to inspire him
Oh, how she longed for his affection
Time passes,
Love fades
True to heart in this pivotal age
Ships push & pull,
Water caresses the shore
Aching bodies tie ropes & more
Broken hearts
Lonesome beds
Rusty chains
Underfed

She employs a new tactic
& maneuvers her hand to his thigh

We are all blind beggars in the cold calculus
of night

CHAPTER IV

Can we agree on something?

Life,
The awkward moment
Between birth & death
Human bones ground down
Until there's nothing left
The greed of excess,
Disguised
As a desire for progress
The death of a generation
Igniting the fury that is now

Passion pulls one way,
Survival another
Young people
Soldiers & protestors
Manipulated by the dog men
Our elected officials
Getting high on that bone blow,
Addicted to well-wishing
& casting stones

CHAPTER V

(Train whistle blows)
Engine rumbles down the track
Smoke pours heroic black
Running strategically behind the barrio
Low-income patrons file into the depot
Collage of last season's clothes
Second-hand hats, shirts & gloves,
I see you
Summer dress
Suitcase
Luxurious repose
She's coming with me,
I'm taking her home

CHAPTER VI

My wild love
Master of day's cool horizon
Religion has no foundation in your eyes

I want to mean so much to you
I want to startle you like thunder
I want to slip into a stoned slumber with you
& never wake up

CHAPTER VII

(View of an empty city street)
Time lapse
(Street is now bustling)
Broken glass,
Cracked concrete,
Dog eating from a trashcan
Rich girls,
Poor boys
Wild vagrant dance,
Shell games,
Boutique shops
The monk in a trance
(Nightfall & neon lights)
Cue jazz beat

CHAPTER VIII

I want to feel real
Like cool, evening rain
Not some feeble surrogate,
Tolerating pain
Wading languidly in the dream pool's shallow end,
Never diving into the depths of lament

I'm sick of darkness,
Am I alone?
Sick of lies,
Suited men casting stones
Have they no knowledge,
Wisdom,
Aplomb?
Play, piano, play
Make thy voice known

Give us credence,
A reason
We used to believe
& receive
Things of wisdom
Redeem us
Oh, my desert flower
Blooming calmly
In a strange, dry hour
I wept over you
Day & night
My tears nourishing & nurturing
My voice giving light

Give us parchment
& a pen
Grant us mercy
& a bed
I feel we existed
More elegantly before
My nightmare came true
Upon opening the door
Snakes
Suits
Medicine men

War generals cling
To a speech writers pen
Promising
Hoping
Amber waves of grain
Pigeon-holing freedom
Expediting graves
"Line up to receive your murder"
Uncle Sam put a gun to my head and told me
he loved me

CHAPTER IX

"What's that down there?" she asked
"I don't know, looks like . . . hope."

Comedians
Minstrels
Bandits of truth
Romantics
Artists
& bleeding hearts
Poets
Thespians
Newborn worshippers
& worthy ministers
All parading as an elegant bride
Down Division Street

CHAPTER X

Could our reality be any more hellish than now?
& real

We despise that dark hand
Always working, lurking in the shadows
Always weaving a web,
Closing off the tombs
Young girls bring flowers & perfume,
Remembering the dead

The hand that ignites,
Provokes,
Spurs us on,
Assigns our number,
& judges our wrongs
Dollars per hour
Lives per gallon
Isn't it good to know how much we are worth?

CHAPTER XI

Evening
Crisp nightfall
I saw her
Buxom half-breed,
Born to roam
She called herself pestilence
Game of chance
With polished chrome

Her face, European at a glance
Yet something different from another angle

She addresses me as if I know her,
"Why don't you hold me in the vacant scene of
night?"
"I'm afraid to"
"Why?"
"Scrutiny, persecution, religion, death . . . should I
go on?"

CHAPTER XII

Is free thinking out of season?
Is slavery the next big thing?
What made the front page this week . . . young
blood?
T.V. commercials selling you remedies to get your
wound well
What of the wound
How did you come by it?
Tell me how it found you,
Please do tell

Famous white citadel
The height of luxury
Scrutiny
Warmongers
Shit hoarders
Plague salesmen
Keeping our soldiers dead
Obese children fed
Their dour glances
Are like a tear gas
Their gibberish,
A drunken mass
Brooklyn needs a hero,
Manhattan a soul

CHAPTER XIII

Sorry for waking you, Lazarus
Did you have a good sleep?
A good dream?
I've been worried about you
It's time to rise

CHAPTER XIV

Painkillers
Nervous thirst
Red ink
Funeral hearse
I found her, the girl
Outside a bar on Division Street
Drunk
Beaten
Dead
Escaped
I found a needle near the body
Red, white & blue letters read,
"Made in China/Born in Japan"
Uncle Sam forced her to inject chemical weapons
into her life
& then he made her his wife

CHAPTER XV

Get my lumber from the King's forest

CHAPTER XVI

A world on fire
Collection of faces
Staring, cheering, changing slowly
All types of gathering together
Insane freedom cries
The bell tolls, it rings for new life
Hear the dogs bark
Ignore their calls
As the magicians rise,
The empire falls
Come on now,
Just a little further
Borders are meant
To be passed over
Cross the street like a fearless child,
Hand-in-hand
With your father sky
& Mother Earth

CHAPTER XVII

The world is ours, cried the movie director
Burn your scripts, it's all over
Do you like having wings on your shoulders?
I'm a winged creature now
& you are my careless lover
Standing
Observing
With one leg in the water,
The other on the land

Let me sing you my song
Let me love you until I'm gone
Come with me, oh please come along
I promise this won't take long
Paradise lost
& paradise found
Listen . . .
Can you hear the distant, echoing sound?

CHAPTER XVIII

(Strike up the band. Slow, chugging, soft blues)

Stay away from my heart, baby
Steer clear of my shore
Stay away from my heart, baby
You'll only hurt me more

Don't come looking for me, baby
Down by the pier
Don't come looking for me, baby
You'll only bring me to tears

(Sharp, piercing harmonica solo)

Leave me to my own now, baby
I ain't trying to hide
Leave me to my own now, baby
At the winding riverside

POSTLUDE

Let me leave you with this
My friend, my love, my visitor
Stand at the door & knock
Yes, stand at the door & knock
Mercy abides & forgiveness resides
Don't fear the day of reckoning
The crimson night shall clear the path for you
Go now, depart
& may God's love go with you
Glory as a divine agent
Peace among you,
Hopeful squire
Stand your ground,
Don't forget me
Breathe deeply
I love you,
The End

www.ingramcontent.com/pod-product-compliance
Lightning Source LLC
Chambersburg PA
CBHW070803050426
42452CB00012B/2476
* 9 7 8 1 9 4 4 3 1 3 0 8 1 *